Looking Unto JESUS

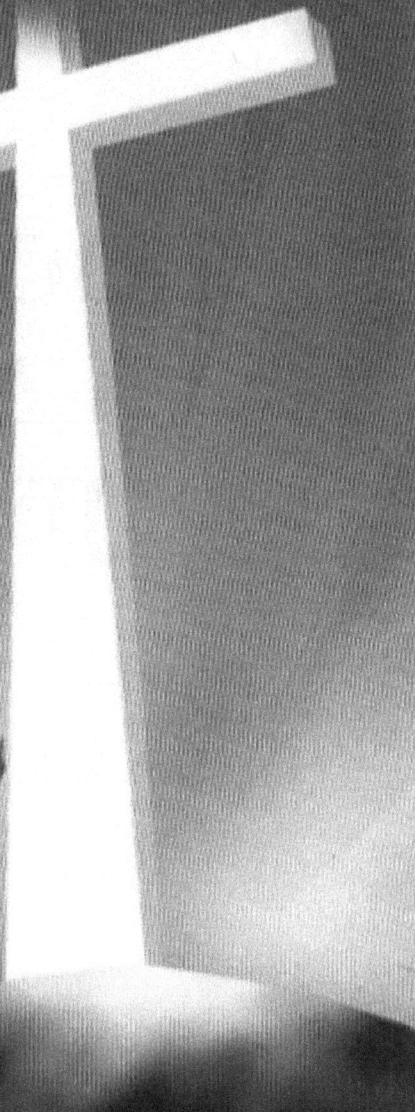

Dr. D. K. Olukoya

LOOKING UNTO JESUS

DR. D.K. OLUKOYA

LOOKING UNTO JESUS
© 2010 DR. D. K. OLUKOYA
ISBN 978-978-8424-27-7
December 2010

Published by:
The Battle Cry Christian Ministries
322, Herbert Macaulay Way, Yaba P. O. Box 12272, Ikeja, Lagos.
email: battlecrysales@mountainoffire.org
Phone: 2348033044239

All Scripture quotation is from the King James Version of the Bible

All rights reserved.
We prohibit reproduction in whole or part without written permission.

CONTENTS

LOOKING UNTO JESUS	5
DIVINE ENCOUNTER	9
THE POWER OF THE CROSS	15
JESUS NEVER FAILS	21
NOT BY BREAD ALONE	25
CANDIDATES OF HEAVEN AND HELL	33
ARE YOU A CANDIDATE OF HEAVEN?	39
OTHER BOOKS BY DR. D. K. OLUKOYA	47

CHAPTER ONE

LOOKING UNTO JESUS

"To the law and to the testimony: if they speak not according to this word, it is because there is no light in them." Isaiah 8:20:

In a nutshell, what that verse is saying is that as far as what you are saying is not in accordance with the word of God, there is no light in you. The Bible says, "Jesus is the only true light that lighteth every man that comes into the world." It also says that in Him is light and that light is the light of men and it is that light that shines in darkness, and darkness cannot even understand it let alone overcome it.

One thing we should all know, is that man is a religious creature. Whenever there is anything to be worshiped, you can be sure you will find men there worshiping the thing. So you should not be surprised when you see men worshiping stones or even rims of tyres or candles or rivers.

If you make a list of all the idols that we have in Nigeria alone, you will write a mighty book. Even, if you pick those in only one town, they are sufficient for a big book. So, basically, man is a religious creature. Unfortunately, beloved, much of the tragedies we have experienced in the world could be linked one way or the other to the religious nature of man.

This is why we say that Christianity is not a religion. In religion, man believes in the existence of a God, a super being, for whom you have to perform certain rites in order to please. But Christianity is God's way of seeking to save the lost.

The religious act of man has caused him a lot of trouble and it is so sad, when you see a lot of people doing things they believe so religiously but they are wrong.

Several years ago, I was somewhere in Harare for a conference. I noticed that every time we sat in the dining hall, a nice lady sat beside me. She would do the sign of the cross and pray quietly over her food. No other person was praying in that hall. She had a large cross over her neck and a rosary and I was impressed. When we got talking, she talked to me about science and all kinds of things and I told her about Jesus. One day, she said, "This your prayer that you have been talking about, maybe we should pray tonight." I said, "That would be very nice." We sat down and I called one prayer point.

As we prayed, she suddenly started shouting: "Stop praying! Stop praying. rding me."oun Oh, look at these beautiful girls surI said, "Beautiful girls? Where are they?" "Oh, can't you see?" she said. And I said, "These are not beautiful girls, they are demon spirits, I cannot see any beautiful girl here but since you say they are here, let them receive the fire of God, in the name of Jesus." She said, 'No, don't harm them." Here was a religious person following all the rules of religion but yet, she was seriously possessed by all kinds of spirits.

Religion is something that the devil likes so much because it does not affect him in any way. As long as that religion is lifeless, the devil does not mind, you can do everything you want to do. For example, the devil does not mind if you build big altars and fill them with the bones of dead men. If you have very nice pews and pulpits as long as it is dead men that are ministering there, the devil does not mind.

If you paint the pictures of all the angels on the walls, as far as the people worshiping there are dead, the devil does not mind. If you have doctorate degree in Theology or Masters in Bible Knowledge, as far as you are dead, the devil does not mind. I was invited to a church many years ago. When I got there, I noticed that they did not pray much in that church. So I said, "In this church, I know that you don't pray much but today we shall pray differently."

After a very short message, I asked them, "Are you now ready to pray?" They said they were ready. We started to pray but within a few minutes somebody came in by the door and spoke in good English : "Stop it, stop it. We don't pray like this here. Stop it. Where is the bell?" I did not know him so I tapped one of the ladies who was busy praying and asked, "Who is this man?" "That's our pastor," she said, "But me, I'm not going to stop." I was so embarrassed.

The ladies refused to stop. I banged the bench, they didn't stop. They just went on. When the man saw that they did not stop, he walked out in anger and the next Sunday service, he dealt with them. That time I had gone. The sad thing was that the man who said we should stop praying had problem with his kidney and he died two weeks later. Probably if he had put religion aside and had allowed those ladies to pray for him his case would have been different.

A lot of people are very religious but God is not interested in religion. He wants the reality inside your heart. Look at the number of people who have been caged and tortured. Many homes have been shattered and many young children have lost their lives in religious crusades. Because of religion twins were being killed in some parts of Nigeria before Mary Slessor came. Many people die because their religion forbids them from eating nutritious foods.

Sometime ago, one woman, who was coming to our fellowship, gave birth to a baby and suddenly we found that she was looking malnourished. We asked her what the problem was. She said, "Ah, in my husband's family, according to their idol, when you are delivered of a baby, the only food you could eat for about two months was gari soaked in water before you could start eating proper food, and palm-oil or groundnut oil must never be added to the woman's food. The Bible says, "Be as quiet as a dove and as wise as a serpent." So we made an arrangement, whenever the woman came to the service we prepared good food for her and she ate before she went home to take her gari. That was religion.

Many potentially useful young men have been rendered useless by religion. The other day, I was at Oshodi, Lagos and I saw some young men who scrapped their hair leaving a little bit at the centre of their head.

They were beating drums and jumping up and I wondered endlessly why they were doing what they were doing. It was because of religion. Some people are poor because their religion wants them to be poor. Religion makes men blind. We have a lot of religious men and traditionalists coming to church and God wants to deliver them from that spirit for God hates religion with perfect hatred.

CHAPTER TWO
DIVINE ENCOUNTER

"And Jacob was left alone; and there wrestled a man with him until the breaking of the day. And when he saw that he prevailed not against him, he touched the hollow of his thigh; and the hollow of Jacob's thigh got out of joint, as he wrestled with him. And he said, Let me go for the day breaketh. And he said, I will not let thee go, except thou bless me. And he said unto him, What is thy name? And he said, Jacob. And he said, Thy name shall be called no more Jacob, but Israel: for as a prince hast thou power with God and with men, and hast prevailed. And Jacob asked him, and said, Tell me I pray thee, thy name. And he said, Wherefore is it that thou dost ask after my name? And he blessed him there. And Jacob called the name of the place Peniel: for I have seen God face to face, and my life is preserved. And as he passed over Penuel, the sun rose upon him, and he halted upon his thigh."
Genesis 32:2–31

A closer look at this simple passage reveals great lessons to be learned from Jacob's encounter:

1. **The power of prevailing prayer.** It shows that you can pray until you prevail.

2. **The long leg of Jacob that was used for evil had to be dislocated so that he could rely on God.**

3. **When you see the Lord, remarkable changes come upon your life.**
No one who has had an encounter with God will remain the same. I always pray that God will show the vision of heaven to Christians and also the vision of hell fire, so that they can see the difference.

When they see both, they can then take the decision whether to go to that place where worms of fire are coming out of people's noses or where there is music and joy. The Bible says, "Ears have not heard, eyes have not seen, it has not even entered into the imagination of man what God has planned for His people." You have to make up your mind where you want to be. I shall be in heaven by God's grace. When a sinner meets God, or God meets a sinner, something must happen and it must be permanent. Maybe you haven't had any encounter with God.

The story of Jacob is telling you that you must have a personal encounter with God. If you do not have a personal encounter with God, then you are a religious person. You are just going to church. You can confess your sins to any priest or pastor.

You can be confirmed twice. You can even sew mini wedding dress, you are still a religious person. You are not going anywhere. When you have an encounter with God, your life changes; it will be an unforgettable thing. When others are saying, "I'm even tired, I want to backslide," you will say, "Ah, me, I dare not after what I've seen, I dare not."

I could remember a church in England where women wore skirts and never came to church in trousers. They covered their hair when they prayed and it was a white man's church. There was a time I was the only black person there and the members were so nice and loving. One day, after service, they surrounded me and were singing, "Happy birthday to you." I first thought I was hearing the voice of angels, then when I heard 'Daniel' I checked my wrist watch and found that the day was my birthday. They had memorised it even though I had forgotten.

Religion is not what we are talking about but the reality of people's personal encounter with God. You will remember when you meet Him. You have been hearing of Him by the hearing of the ear but when you meet Him like Isaiah did, nobody needs to tell you how bad you are. You will know and you will adjust yourself very quickly. If you do not have that kind of encounter, everything you are doing now may still be religion. I am praying that, the Lord will deliver you today, in Jesus' name. You can be confirmed twice. You can even sew mini wedding dress, you are still a religious person. You are not going anywhere

When you have an encounter with God, your life changes; it will be an unforgettable thing. When others are saying, "I'm even tired, I want to backslide," you will say, "Ah, me, I dare not after what I've seen, I dare not." I could remember a church in England where women wore skirts and never came to church in trousers. They covered their hair when they prayed and it was a white man's church.

There was a time I was the only black person there and the members were so nice and loving. One day, after service, they surrounded me and were singing, "Happy birthday to you." I first thought I was hearing the voice of angels, then when I heard 'Daniel' I checked my wrist watch and found that the day was my birthday. They had memorised it even though I had forgotten.

Religion is not what we are talking about but the reality of people's personal encounter with God. You will remember when you meet Him. You have been hearing of Him by the hearing of the ear but when you meet Him like Isaiah did, nobody needs to tell you how bad you are. You will know and you will adjust yourself very quickly. If you do not have that kind of encounter, everything you are doing now may still be religion. I am praying that, the Lord will deliver you today, in Jesus' name We are not talking about where you were born or who your father is. As far as the Bible is concerned, that is completely irrelevant. There were so many people in the Bible who were godly sons of godless fathers and we also have godless sons of godly fathers. There are both camps, so what you should now pursue is where you want to be in God. Ask yourself, "What am I achieving in God?" If for example as you are reading this book, Jesus walks in and says, "Beloved, your time is up, what you have done is enough, come up!" Are you confident that you will go to heaven? That is the most important question.

When you have a personal encounter with God, it is not a question of looking at God from far away; He would be close to you. When you see the appearance of the Lord, there must be a remarkable change in your life. Every self-interest, self-ambition and worldly ambition will die.

Your focus will change, your priority will change. Your life will be revived. You will stop pursuing what you were pursuing before for a new thing. You will undergo a complete revision. Like somebody revises a book; that is how your life will be revised. What makes other people happy will not move you anymore. What would make you happy is your addiction to the Lord your God and the knowledge that at the end of the day you will reign with Jesus. Recently, I got one of the best letters that has ever been written to me.

The person wrote me about two pages. He said, "Dr. Olukoya, we thank God for MFM. All I want to say is this: although I don't have money, I have joy and that joy cannot be explained." He said that he knew that with that joy in his heart, it was a matter of time, every other thing would work well."

4. **The infirmity of Jacob meant that he had to lean on God.**
We too have to lean on God. Now, instead of learning the lessons that God wants us to learn from this message, let us see what men have done. Verse 32 says, "Therefore the children of Israel eat not of the sinew which shrank, which is upon the hollow of the thigh unto this day: because he touched the hollow of Jacob's thigh in the sinew that shrank." Men have turned this to religion. They say, "Don't eat that part of the leg, just as they have turned Good Friday to religion. They say, "Don't eat meat or eat fish on Good Friday." Some American churches have revised this. They say that you can eat meat but not much. What has eating of meat got to do with the crucifixion of our Lord Jesus Christ? Absolutely nothing. Some cook a special meal for that day and some believers go and eat it with them. I am saying all these, to let you know how men turn things to religion.

CHAPTER THREE
THE POWER OF THE CROSS

The cross is not the symbol of Christianity. An empty tomb or tongue of fire is the symbol of Christianity. If Jesus had remained on the cross, all of us would have been finished. But thank God He died and rose from the dead.

If you study church history and read your Bible, you would discover that the early Christians never considered the cross as a honourable symbol. To them, it was a device of death and shame. The disciples never trusted in the cross as an object, but they trusted in what accompanied the cross. They never hung crosses on their necks. All the hanging of cross on the neck took off from paganism. To make matters worse, the word 'Easter' comes from the name of a pagan idol, the idol they claim was responsible for the light of the day. So, it has nothing to do with Christianity.

According to Numbers 21:8, the children of Israel had misbehaved and something had happened. Punishment will normally follow when you make God the tail and you make yourself the head. When God says this is what He wants you to do and you say, "Oh no, I want to do something else, punishment will follow because He knows more than you. Let us recall the story from

> *"And the Lord sent fiery serpents upon the people, and they bit the people and much people of Israel died. Therefore the people came to Moses, and said, we have sinned, for we have spoken against the Lord and against thee; Pray unto the Lord, that He take away the serpents from us. And Moses*

prayed for the people. And the Lord said unto Moses, make thee a fiery serpent, set it upon a pole and it shall come to pass, that everyone that is bitten, when he looketh upon it, he shall live." Numbers 21: 6 - 8

There are lots of lessons too to pick from here. We shall look at the lessons later. In John 3, Jesus made an interesting reference to this incident.

The lifting up of the serpent. It was serpent that was biting them; it was serpent they were told to look unto. Many died because it did not make sense to them. They would have complained thus: "Snake is biting us, they say we should be looking at snake to be saved." But God did not ask you to rationalize or think about it until it becomes logical. If you are going to be rationalizing, forget the supernatural, forget true Christianity. All God is asking you to do is look. He did not say 'think,' but 'look' and once you look, you will be saved. So, this story teaches us many lessons.

1. It speaks of Christ becoming sin for us that we may be made righteous.

2. It speaks of looking upward and living.

3. It speaks of God's power to deliver.

4. It tells us just to believe. Don't try to rationalise. If you start thinking: How can a brazen serpent heal? Then you will be in trouble.

5. It tells us that the world having been bitten by that old serpent has its only cure in Jesus. So, it was a shadow of something that was to come, and the Son of man like that serpent was lifted up; and all He requires from you now is to just look. Fix your eyes on Jesus. But again instead of learning these facts, what did men do?

> *"He removed the high places, and break the images, and cut down the groves, and break in pieces the brazen serpent that Moses had made: for unto those days, the children of Israel did burn incense to it and he called it Nehushtan."*
> 2 Kings 18:4

Instead of understanding what God wanted to teach them about the brazen serpent, men turned it upside down to religion. There are so many examples like that. Do you know that there are beautiful lessons to learn from the slaying of Goliath by David who used Goliath's sword to cut off his head?

1. The sword of the enemy shall be turned against the enemy because the Bible says, "No weapon that is formed against me shall prosper." and the Son of man like that serpent was lifted up; and all He requires from you now is to just look. Fix your eyes on Jesus. But again instead of learning these facts, what did men do?

> *"He removed the high places, and break the images, and cut down the groves, and break in pieces the brazen serpent that Moses had made: for unto those days, the children of Israel did burn incense to it and he called it Nehushtan."*
> 2 Kings 18:4

Instead of understanding what God wanted to teach them about the brazen serpent, men turned it upside down to religion. There are so many examples like that. The cross that was used by satan to kill Jesus became a weapon against satan himself. But by the next time David wanted to use the sword of Goliath, they had wrapped it up; they had turned it to religion.

The events in the life of Christ can be divided into three:

1. **The wonderful way He was born.** There was no ceremony attached to it. It was through His birth that our present calendar was divided into two. Angels came when He was born and the glory shone all around. Only a few shepherds and some animals witnessed His birth.

2. **His death.** The day He died all the angels ran away. God the Father too turned His back. People ridiculed him: "You saved others, now save yourself," they jeered. A large number of crowd watched the trial, the verdict, the crucifixion and the death but very few watched the birth. When he resurrected too, only a few Roman guards and one or two women were able to see him one incident that actually put a sealing on our faith was what happened the

day He died on the cross. There was darkness at an unusual hour, the ground shook and satanic powers were defeated. However, on that day, the angels that announced His birth, that protected Him as a child; that ministered to him in the wilderness, that ministered to him in the Garden of Gethsemane, that came to roll away the stone later, that announced the resurrection, all ran away. The It was a very important event. It was because of this, that we have what is written in

"Looking unto Jesus the author and finisher of our faith who for the joy that was set before him, endured the cross, despising the shame, and sat down at the right side of the throne of God."
Hebrews 12:2

Disaster follows, when you fix your eyes on other things apart from Jesus. Peter tried it and he almost sank. Jesus Himself said that as the serpent was lifted up in the wilderness, so must the Son of man be lifted up. When you look, you shall be saved. What does that "looking" mean? It means to focus your attention on Jesus as your example. When you focus on Him as your example and as your physician, you shall be made whole. If you focus your attention on Him as a teacher, you shall be taught. If you focus your attention on Him as your comforter, you shall be encouraged. If you focus your attention on Him as your strength, you will never be made weak. If you focus your attention on Him as your life, then you have what is called abundant life. That is why the Bible says, "Look unto me and be saved."

Fix your eyes on Jesus. Don't fix your eyes on man. Man can fail you at any moment. The Bible says, the only person that you can trust all the time, is Jesus. When you have too much to do, fix your attention on Jesus. When you know it seems as if things are a little bit rough, don't take your eyes off Jesus. When you fix your eyes on Jesus, everything like loneliness, frustration and depression will fly away. When there is no mother or father to love you, if you fix attention on Jesus, He will look after you. When others disappoint you, Jesus will take care of you.

I remember a sister: on her wedding day, the service was supposed to start by 9 a.m. Between 10 a.m. and noon they expected the bridegroom and he did not show up. The man of God who was getting impatient asked, "Are you sure this man wants to come for this wedding?" "I saw him last night.

We had our bachelor's eve. He's supposed to be here," the bride replied. Eventually, the man did not come. At exactly 1 p.m. somebody decided to go and look for him at home. He did not find him there but he found somebody who said he left a message that he had gone to play tennis. They went there and found him playing lawn-tennis. "Ah, Mister, they're waiting for you in the church," they told him. He said, "Eh, I decided to ditch it, I'm not interested again."

The man who was sent to look for him said, "But if you're not interested, why don't you just go there and say so?" He retorted, "If they don't see me, they will go home." And they did. The man of God said, "This wedding is postponed for circumstances beyond our control." In fact, the bride-to-be was carried home half dead. Some people were pouring cold water on the head of her mother who had invited the Morning Star society of her church to accompany her to the wedding. It was a good thing the Morning Star people were around for they were the people that revived her.

The sister then decided to fix her eyes on Jesus and did not give up. She did not die as some people were expecting and she refused to drink acid. As she fixed her eyes on Jesus, things became clear one day. She realized that the Lord had a purpose and that it was good that the wedding did not take place because within two months from that time, the bridegroom to be died under mysterious circumstances. This sister is now married because her attention was fixed on Jesus.

So, when you are sad, look unto Jesus. If there was a country with internal unrest, such a country would not be able to face an attack from outside. If a believer is sad, there is problem from the inside, so when attack from the outside comes, he will not be able to fight because already there are spies inside. So, fix your eyes on Jesus, even when you are dissatisfied, when you are afraid or when people misunderstand or maltreat you.

When you are struggling financially, fix your eyes on Jesus. Do not fix your eyes on yourself. If you are looking at yourself, you will get into more trouble. Don't fix your eyes on man because you don't know what others are doing. Don't fix your eyes on your trouble because if you do, you will sink. Don't fix your eyes on the devil too, because the devil is looking for who will give him some attention. Don't fix your eyes on false hopes; let your hope be in the Lord.

CHAPTER FOUR
JESUS NEVER FAILS

You will not receive any forgiveness, if you are forever focusing on the sins you have repented from. Somebody needing deliverance will not receive deliverance by buying books on deliverance and by reading about demons. That is not what will get a person out. What will get the person out is ministration.

Some people make the mistake of always looking backward. When you look backward, you are living in the past. You must refuse to live in the past. How can you come to the house of God and allow one mistake you made 15 years ago to spoil the rest of your future. Some people come and say, "Please, help me, 15 years ago, I was sexually abused. This is why I am having problems." "Has God not forgiven you?" I would usually ask. They would say, "Yes." "Have you gone for any deliverance?" "In fact, I did three." "Then what is the problem now?" "Well, I just feel that nothing is happening." How can you allow a mistake you made 15 years ago to be directing your present life? You must refuse to live in the past. Paul said, "Forgetting those things that are behind and looking forward..."

This is one of the successes of Joseph. He refused to live in the past. He rejected the temptation to harbour resentment against his brothers. Many spoil the whole of their lives by carrying wounds and grudges about past events. They remember the way somebody treated them many years ago. With the ugly roots of bitterness inside, their lives do not bear fruits and they are wondering why. How can it bear fruit when there is root of bitterness inside? Beloved, if at any point in time in your life, you have said, "If it had not been for so, so and so, my life would not have been like this," then, you are living in the past. You may have been unjustly treated but you must determine to leave the past behind and walk along.

Do not be the kind of woman who would say, "After my husband had turned me to second hand, then he abandoned me." Who told you that you are second hand? Do not be the kind of child who would say: "It's my daddy. My daddy chased away all my mummy's children and my step-mother stopped our education." You are living in the past. Do not be the kind of girl who would say: "It's my parents: they made me lose the best husband I would have married." That is already gone. Yesterday is too late. Why do you want to worry your spirit about that? As long as you live in the past, you will never be a successful person because that root of bitterness will spoil everything for you. You must forgive and forget. You must do all things without grumbling and complaining.

Some people too are experts at looking at unfavorable circumstances. They forget about Peter who was studying the waves and began to sink. All he needed to do was to face Jesus. As long as you focus your attention on Him and keep following Him, you will be secured. When Peter took his eyes off Jesus, he started to sink.

People sink when they take their eyes off the Lord and look at somebody else. Somebody could go to a house fellowship and simply because he found the leader eating alligator pepper and kola-nut and drinking beer, he would say, "Ah, because of this I won't serveGod again." Such a person is looking at circumstances. Don't do that. Fix your eyes on Jesus. When you fix your eyes on Him, you can never go wrong. It is when we take our eyes off Him and begin to look at ourselves and at other people's mistakes, that we get into trouble.

One problem that so many people will receive judgment for is this: when others are struggling to serve the Lord and are doing their best and you just stand at the back, doing nothing but saying, "It is wrong, it should have been done like this or like that," you make yourself a spiritual referee and as far as God is concerned, He is pleased with the people struggling. It is you that is not impressed. Your not being impressed does not matter as far as God is concerned. As far as God is impressed with the people, He cannot be concerned with what you think. If God is for you, it does not matter who is against you; but if God is against you, nobody can help you.

Some people try to protect themselves so much that they wear bullet-proof vests and build their walls high with barb wires. What they forget is that there are thousands of things that can walk into their houses without bothering to open any gate. They can walk through the wall. Barbed wires cannot prevent demons from walking in. There was a brother that a demon walked to and called by his first name that nobody used to call him. The demon said: "I have been sent to deal with you." The brother said, "In Jesus' name you made a mistake." And light came from heaven on the demon and it grew weak and ran away. The house had a security system at the gate yet the demon came in. Fix your eyes on Jesus. Don't fix your eyes on your problem because that is what satan wants you to do. Anytime you fix your eyes on your problem and pamper it, he is happy. Fix your eyes on Jesus and see what God can do. By sitting down to ponder and worry about your circumstances, you achieve nothing. By allowing the circumstances to discourage you, you achieve nothing. By looking at the roughness of the weather, you achieve nothing. Sometimes, when we say, pray, some people would be busy meditating on their problems. When the message is being preached, they would be meditating on their problems. During the Praise-worship session, they would meditate on their problems. After the service, they continue to meditate on their problems regardless of the powerful manifestations during the service. They do not play any active role in their deliverance. They want it automatically. You must play a role. The Bible says, "Without faith, it is impossible to please God."

It is like somebody who came for the baptism in the Holy Spirit. She prayed and nothing happened. I said, "Why now?" She said, "I have a feeling that somebody will drop something like a radio transistor inside me and the radio transistor would be talking." I said, "It's not so. If a radio transistor is talking inside your tummy, that is a demon. But for the Holy Spirit, you will be the one that will be talking while the Spirit gives you utterance." She said, "If that is so, sir, pray for me."

I prayed and she began to pray in tongues. After she did that for about 20 minutes, she sat down and was looking worried again. I said, "Madam, what is the matter again?" She said, "Why am I not rolling on the floor like those people?" I asked her, "Why do you want to roll on the floor? Those people are possessed." She said, "But they are rolling on the floor. I too want to roll on the floor." She was looking at circumstances forgetting that circumstances can discourage one.

Take your eyes off them. What we call faith sometimes looks like madness. When you look at circumstances and you begin to envy other people, you forget that God's plans for our individual lives are different. Don't work by other peoples' time-table. "Looking unto Jesus," the Bible says, "the author and finisher of our faith."

Beloved, pray for that grace to fix your eyes on Jesus and on Him alone, not on the pastor, not on the house fellowship leader, not on the group leader.

PRAYER POINT

1. O Lord, give me the grace to fix my eyes upon you all the time, in the name of Jesus.

CHAPTER FIVE
NOT BY BREAD ALONE

Beloved, the Bible talks about the sower who in his assignment, had some of his seeds fell on good ground and yielded bountifully while some fell on barren land and therefore yielded nothing. God wants to profit with us hence He is investing in our lives.

You cannot afford to live the life of an unprofitable servant, who buried the one talent that was given to him by his master. This means that your life must be tailored towards yielding dividends unto God. At this juncture, I want you to raise your voice and pray: "O Lord, anything that will not make You to profit with my life, take it out now, in the name of Jesus."

> *"Then was Jesus led up of the spirit into the wilderness to be tempted of the devil. And when he had fasted forty days and forty nights, he was afterward an hungred. And when the tempter came to him, he said, If thou be the Son of God, command that these stones be made bread. But he answered and said, It is written, Man shall not live by bread alone, but by every word that proceedeth out of the mouth of God."*
> Matthew 4:1-4

For you to remain standing as a Christian who will make heaven, there are three things you cannot put aside:

1. **Holiness**: The Bible does not mince words as regards the importance of holiness. It says in Hebrews 12: 14: "Follow peace with all men, and holiness, without which

no man shall see the Lord:" You may see anything, you may see vision, you may prophesy, you may know your pastor, you can hold all the church posts but seeing God without being holy is impossible.

2. **Prayer:** Jesus did not say preach without ceasing, but He said pray without ceasing. Without prayer, you cannot communicate with God. This is a nonnegotiable condition for making heaven. A prayerless Christian is a dead Christian. The staff with which to walk with God is prayer.

3. **The word of God:** This is one area where the devil has dealt a serious blow on so many Christians. It is sad but true that many church goers are completely ignorant of the Bible. I am not talking about the theoretical experiences many gain from Bible colleges. You could even go to these colleges and come out more confused.

Many church goers are even completely ignorant of whom the Lord really is. Some would resolve to read the Bible from cover to cover only to abandon it midway. To some, the best place for their Bible is under the pillow, with a Psalm opened, and to some, it is a tool to be used when in danger. Many have small Bibles; some have big ones but do not read them.

Without any argument, we all know that the Bible has changed so many lives. In countries where reading the Bible has for long been accepted as tradition, progress was rapid. While in places where people do not like to read the Bible, progress has been slow. Those who read it before but later abandoned it, are in trouble now. There is power in the Word of God, if not, there would not have been so many attempts to destroy it.

Perhaps you have heard of John Wycliffe, the first man to translate the Bible to English. Prior to his effort, only priests or pastors used to read the Bible and their interpretation of it was unquestionable. John Wycliffe's efforts were therefore seen as a threat to this situation. No wonder he was eventually killed for making it possible for everyone to read the Bible. They killed him, but even some years after his death, they were still not satisfied with the punishment of death. So, his corpse was exhumed and burnt to ashes and the ashes were dumped inside the river.

Happily today, the Bible is everywhere and in it, we have the best of books, the greatest book and the most wonderful book. It is the book that has lasted longer than any other book. It is however sad to note that it is the most neglected book. A lot of people do not know that when they do not read the Word of God to feed their spirits, they will have no strength spiritually.

There was a man in a country where they do not permit people to read Bible. His only Bible was seized and thrown away. Later, he discovered that somebody else had one hidden in a village nearby. He managed to get in touch with him and started copying about two chapters a day. Two chapters were sent to his son and by the time he was through with it, he got born again. It is amazing to see many in a free country as ours still refusing to read the Bible and get filled with the powers therein.

In a certain place, a man was preaching at the back of the house of a university professor. He described the birth of Jesus Christ - how a virgin gave birth to a son called Jesus. Hearing this, the professor was upset and described his sermon as illogical, because to him, there was no way a virgin could give birth. To further discredit the sermon and the Bible as a whole, he bought a copy of the New Testament and studied it for thirteen years. By the time he was through with it, he became a born again child of God. It was then his turn to preach the Word with even greater fire than that of the man he set out to discredit. Such, is the power in the word.

It is not only prayers that you need to get along with God. In fact, when your prayers are devoid of the Word of God, the devil will not respect you much. Remember he was defeated by Jesus with the weapon of "It is written." Recently, a sister recently paid dearly for her low level of the Word. She saw a demon in the dream who showed a part of her body to her and said to her, "You are not going to get it." She then started quoting the Scriptures against the demon. To her amazement, the demon demanded from her where the quoted Scriptures were written in the Bible but she could not tell. This delayed her miracle for some time but that incident taught her a lesson. The Bible commands that we should keep God's words in own hearts.

> *"And these words, which I command thee this day, shall be in thine heart." Deuteronomy 6:6*
> *"Thy word have I hid in mine heart, that I might not sin against thee." Psalm 119:11*

This implies that it is possible for you to hear the Word and the devil takes it away. So, there must be a determined effort on your part to hide the word in your heart. To do this, two things are required:

1. **Kick all useless thoughts out of your heart.** Worldly and ungodly thoughts struggle for the same space in the heart with the Word of God. One has to go, for the other to stay. It is the height of hypocrisy for a person to come to the house of God and write down passages quoted by the preachers together with the messages and then never go over them again in his private time. Some even forget their jotters in the house of God, because other irrelevant and worldly thoughts, have occupied their hearts. These must be knocked out for the Word to have a landing place.

2. **Form the habit of meditation.** A starting point is to pick a verse or two a day and meditate on them throughout the day. This is where many miss it. They do not read their Bibles, and do not memorise Scriptures, they are therefore empty. As serious Christians, we are not only supposed to hear the Word of God, read and study it, but we must also memorise and meditate upon it. It is only after that that you can begin to apply it and share it with others. Many are not aware of the fact that the level of the Word inside them is known by the devil. He knows those who are serious Bible students and those who just read the Bible to silence their conscience. He recognizes those who read for the sake of reading. So he can gauge the spiritual temperature of many by the level of the Word in them. John 1:1: "In the beginning was the Word, and the Word was with God, and the Word was God." Verse 14: "And the Word was made flesh, and dwelt among us, (and we beheld his glory, the glory as of the only begotten of the Father) full of grace and truth." A careful analysis of these verses reveal that the Word of God is the Son of God and if the Word dwells in you, then the Son is in you. The opposite is also very true.

3. **Read the whole content of the Word of God:** The Bible says that the word of God is the Son of God. So, for Jesus to dwell richly in your life, the Word must dwell richly in you. The Bible also likened the Word of God to a seed. The parable of the sower talks about some seeds falling on a good soil, some on the rock, etc. The seed talked about here, is the Word of God. Your heart must receive it or else it dies. The Bible also likened the Word of God to a sword.

"For the word of God is quick, and powerful, and sharper than any two-edged sword, piercing even to the dividing asunder of soul and spirit, and of the joints and marrow, and is a discerner of the thoughts and intents of the heart." Hebrew 4:12

The Word of God is a mirror through which you can look at yourself to see the way you are and make adjustment. We are encouraged to know the Bible, which is the Word of God. Anything in you that hates the Bible is your greatest enemy, and that may lead you to hell fire. You are to receive the Word fully. If it says, "Do not," then don't do it. Do not argue, do not use human logic to figure it out. Swallow it, hook, line and sinker. We should dwell in the Word of God. Anybody who has made up his mind not to obey God has no business coming to the house of God because each time you come and God talks to you and you turn your back and go away without making any adjustment, He writes it down and the words will then stand against you on the day of judgment. If you have been born again for five years and you have not read the Bible through once, I put it to you that you are lazy.

Sometimes ago, in England, I preached to a white boy and he gave his life to Jesus. That was on a Tuesday and by the next Tuesday when we were to have our Bible study, he had read through the entire Bible. Yet we had old members of the church who got born again before him but had never for once read through the Bible. When you read the Bible, it quickens you. The Bible says the flesh profits nothing, therefore, when you read the Word, you are strengthened and when you abandon it, you go lean. Beloved, this is the word from God to you. If you have abandoned your Bible, please make amends and it will be well with you. At this juncture, I would like you to bow your head and confess your sins.

If you know you are a lazy Bible reader or you only read the Bible when you feel like or you are one of those who just carry it about, ask the Lord to forgive you and make a covenant with Him that you will be on fire as far as the Word of God is concerned, that you will not allow the enemy to cheat you or put you on the shelf because of the lack of reading the Word of God. Talk to Him and He will surely help you. The Bible says, "Forever O Lord, thy Word is settled in heaven." Also, tell the Lord that the giant of ignorance in your life should die. Ignorance is a serious giant that paralyses people.

Pray: "Everything that the devil has secretly stolen from me because of lack of the knowledge of the Word of God, I claim them back, in the name of Jesus."

> *"Jesus answered and said unto them, Ye do err, not knowing the scriptures, nor the power of God."* Matthew 22:29

Jesus is saying that, not knowing the Scripture nor the power of God will result in error. Ignorance could make a person to be living in sin without knowing it. It is sad and the effect, disastrous. The disciples of Jesus got into very serious confusion in Luke 24:4 which says,

> *"And it came to pass, as they were much perplexed thereabout, behold, two men stood by them in shining garments."* Luke 24:4

They were confused because they had forgotten that Jesus had earlier warned them about looking for the living among the dead. Lack of the knowledge of the Word of God will result in the following:

a. **Spiritual dullness.**

b. **Confusion.** A person who does not know and have the Word of God in him
would be roaming about aimlessly and would suffer unnecessarily. He will be afraid where there is no fear. The devil will kick him about like a football.

c. **Spiritual sickness.** A person without the Word will suffer malnutrition because the Bible is the food for the soul. Many Christians are sick or weak because their spirits too are sick. The physical food that we eat has various functions it carries out in our body.

For example, food builds up our body and replaces worn out tissues in us. Through food you get energy. What food does to our physical body is what the Word of God does to our spirits. Hence in some places, the Bible calls the Word of God milk, bread or honey. Spiritual malnutrition will happen when a person is not feeding adequately on the Word of God.

d. **Lack of spiritual resistance:** An affected will not be able to resist the devil because his spirit lacks the necessary strength.

e. **Sinful life:** Sin will keep you away from the Bible and the Bible will keep you away from sin. Therefore, lack of the Word will keep you in sin.

Beloved, living without the Word of God is empty Christianity. Your life should not be by bread alone. Resolve not to be an empty barrel as far as the Word is concerned. Make a definite plan to saturate your spirit with the Word and ask the Lord to help you. May your Bible reading be revived by fire, in Jesus' name.

PRAYER POINTS

1. I renounce any signature of my name in satanic possession, in the name of Jesus.
2. I release my name, from every satanic possession, in the name of Jesus.
3. I release myself, from any ceremony linking me to evil powers, in the name of Jesus.
4. I release myself, from every blood donation to the devil, in the name of Jesus.
5. I paralyse and disband all satanic parents, in the name of Jesus.
6. I renounce every satanic baptism, in Jesus' name.
Every power, assigned to hide my light under the bed, be paralysed, in the name of Jesus.

CHAPTER FIVE
CANDIDATES OF HEAVEN AND HELL

"There was a certain rich man, which was clothed in purple and fine linen, and fared sumptuously every day. And there was a certain beggar named Lazarus, which was laid at his gate, full of sores. And desiring to be fed with the crumbs which fell from the rich man's table: moreover, the dogs came and licked his sores. And it came to pass, that the beggar died, and was carried by the angels into Abraham's bosom the rich man also died and was buried; And in hell he lift up his eyes, being in torments, and seeth Abraham afar off, and Lazarus in his bosom. And he cried and said, Father Abraham, have mercy on me, and send Lazarus, that he may dip the tip of his finger in water, and cool my tongue; for I am tormented in this flame. But Abraham said, Son, remember that thou in thy lifetime receivedst thy good things, and likewise Lazarus evil things: but now he is comforted, and thou art tormented. And beside all this, between us and you there is a great gulf fixed: so that they which would pass from hence to you cannot; neither can they pass to us, that would come from thence. Then he said, I pray thee therefore, father, that thou wouldest send him to my father's house: For I have five brethren; that he may testify unto them, lest they also come into this place of torment. Abraham said unto him, they have Moses and the prophets, let them hear them. And he said, Nay, father Abraham: but if one went unto them from the dead, they will repent. And he said unto him, if they hear not Moses and the prophets, neither will they be persuaded, though one rose from the dead." Luke 16:19-31

This was not a parable but a real life story told by Jesus. Both men actually existed, for the Bible says there was a certain rich man. There was actually a rich man and there was indeed a Lazarus. Beloved, know today that there is great danger in your not being sure of your salvation. And if you cannot make up your mind which way you are going, you are not sure whether it is heaven or hell, then you are on your way to hell because those on their way to heaven know it. And it is very good to understand these things now.

This message is for two groups of people: those who are candidates for heaven and those who are candidates for hell. You can divide Christians into those two groups any day anytime. In the above story, the rich man died and when he opened his eyes, he found himself in hell fire. Lazarus also died and found himself in the bosom of Abraham. Then the man shouted to father Abraham, "I am tormented in this place, let Lazarus put his hand in water and cool my tongue." Abraham said, "No, it is not possible. There is a great gulf between you and us. You cannot come here. Apart from that, while you enjoyed yourself in the world, Lazarus suffered. So, while you are now suffering, he is enjoying." What Abraham was telling him was that there was no remedy at all.

My prayer is that, you would not push yourself to a stage, where the issues of your life will have no remedy. Saul got to that stage and God said, "I regret making Saul a king. He has disappointed me." Samuel cried to the Lord all night: "Father, please." God said, "Talk no more to me about this matter. I have made up my mind." And that was it. He had got to the point of no return. You may ask, "Why did the rich man go to hell fire?" Luke 16:19: "There was a certain rich man, which was clothed in purple and fine linen, and fared sumptuously every day." Was it because he was rich? No, Abraham was also a rich man. He was rich in cattle and all kinds of things. So, a rich man can make heaven if the money does not become his idol, if he does not place that money above God, and if he learns the principle of giving out, not the principle of hoarding the money.

Did the rich man go to hell because he was clothed in purple and fine linen? No. Being well-dressed is not a sin. Was it because he ate good food? No. Food is useful to the physical body. Was it because he did not look after the beggar at his door? No. No one can look after all the beggars in the world. The reason was that at a stage in his life, he had said no to Jesus repeatedly. People like him would always argue and would have no time for God.

A long time ago, somebody died at the age of 70. Someone analyzed the 70 years he lived. He slept 23 years, worked 16 years, watched television 8 years ate 6 years, spent about 6 years travelling and 4 years on leisure, was ill for 4 years, spent 2 years dressing up, and 2 years on prayer and religious activities. So, this person was a likely candidate for hell fire. Candidates for hell fire can be known by the way they spend their time.

Many of us deceive ourselves. If you go to a big stadium, you will find many people there. If you touch a young man and say, "Who is likely to die first in this place?" He would look for people with grey hair, whereas age does not follow at all. A visit to the mortuary will convince you. Sometimes, you don't find a person with grey hair in a whole mortuary. You may think you have time, but you don't really have time. So, you must take a decision. Do you really have time for Jesus?

Remember that each day we spend here takes us either nearer to heaven or nearer to hell fire. That rich man opened his eyes and found himself in hell fire. Death is a leveller. It levels everybody. It does not recognize the high or the low and it cannot be bribed. You can't give it money. One professor prayed for a child for a long time. Then his wife got pregnant, and then put to bed. They brought the man the news that his wife was delivered of a bouncing baby boy.

He was so happy that he jumped up for joy, and by the time he got down, he was dead. He had what is called rupture of the vessel supplying blood to the brain. And that was it. Another man was shaking hands with his friend, saying, "Congratulations, you have just received a major award." Suddenly, the man found out that his friend was not talking to him again. He was dead. Death is a leveller.

So, this is the time to make yourself worthy of God's calling. The rich man opened his eyes and found himself in hell fire. The Bible does not tell us that there is purgatory, a place which is neither heaven nor hell, and that you can stay there while somebody prays for you in the church and you eventually go to heaven. This is not in the word of God. Somebody who has no time for God but has time to look for money will pay dearly for it.

The rich man had no time for God. His offering was always low. He did not attend fellowship neither did he pray. He did not bother to receive the Holy Spirit. But the other man had time for God, although he was poor. So, how do you spend your time? Time is one of the greatest gifts that God gives to us, and He gives everyone the same quantity of time. Your 60 minutes is my 60 minutes, your 60 seconds is my 60 seconds.

But time is a perishable gift. Once you lose it, you lose it for ever.

Your spiritual power is an indication of how you use your time. A fool may waste money but the greatest fool wastes his time. If somebody wastes 15 minutes every hour, and the person lives 100 years, he would have wasted 25 good years of his life. So, to find out what a man worships and where he is going, study how he spends his time.

Does God have the largest share of your time? If it is money, do you spend most of it in serving God? If you spend your time to sleep with sister 'A' on Monday, B on Tuesday, C on Wednesday and so on till Sunday before you get to your wife at home, you know where you are heading for. Can you account for the way you spend your day? Are you the type who does two hours work in four hours? Or you are the kind of believer who still has the time to be angry? Have you time to be moody, or to be gossiping and complaining? Are you the type of Christian who talks too much, you say 200 words per minute? Do you say useless things or make purposeless visits? Examine how you spend your time. Do unworthy things take up most of your time? Do spiritual things take less of your time? The activities you spend your time on most, will indicate where you are going. Is it prayer? Bible study? Working for Christ? Witnessing or are you always idle?

Are you one of those who worship the god of sleep, the god of entertainment, the god of television, or the god of games? Many people are addicted to television shows and the devil uses that opportunity to plant many arrows into many people's lives because they substitute the time for prayer in watching television.

People who say no to Jesus, are people who refuse to give their lives completely, and they are candidates for hell fire. Remember that life is a one-way street. You can't go back and correct what you have done. There is no repentance in the grave. So, if you keep saying no to Jesus, you will find yourself in hell fire. Judgment will begin in the house of God. It won't begin in the film houses; it won't begin in the house of those who claim to be worshipping the LORD.

In case you have any malice against anybody, go immediately and settle with the person. Tell the person, "You did so, so and so to me and I didn't like it," because if Jesus finds that malice in your heart, you are a candidate for hell fire. No unclean thing shall enter heaven. God loves His people so much that He will not allow a single sinner to enter into heaven with them. The wages of sin is eternal separation from God. God is no respecter of persons and He has no useless activities.

There was a girl, whenever her parents went to church, she showed no interest. She found more pleasure in her boyfriend who was in Form Two. Not quite long this boy put her in a family way. Then the girl said, "I cannot find my menses." The boy said, "Search for it." After three months, it was known that she was pregnant. Then the boy went to one of those local chemists, a person who had no medical experience, and bought a syringe and drugs which they told him to give the girl. After sometime, he asked her, "Have you found the thing?" She said, "I have not found it."

He told her that he had something and the girl who had no time for church services, submitted herself to the boy to administer the injection. Trouble started. They carried her all over the place, and she eventually died. Before her death, she confessed that somebody gave her an injection. Her parents threatened to take the boy to court for manslaughter. But people advised them, "You are wasting your time. Where is the evidence? Who was there when he administered the drug? You better forget it.

Your daughter has gone for good." The girl had no time to follow her parents to church. She had time to go to hell fire. One sin God can never forgive anybody is saying no to Jesus. Are you a candidate for hell fire? You better repent now. There is an opportunity now. Or are you a candidate for heaven?

CHAPTER FIVE
ARE YOU A CANDIDATE OF HEAVEN?

Let us see how to recognise candidates for heaven.

1. **They do the will of God:**

    "Thy kingdom come, Thy will be done in earth, as it is in heaven." So, candidates for heaven are those who do the will of the Father. They don't do their own will. They will not allow the foolish things here to prevent them from getting home. Matthew 6:10

    "And truly, if they had been mindful of that country from whence they came out, they might have had opportunity to have returned. But now they desire a better country, that is an heavenly: wherefore God is not ashamed to be called their God: for he hath prepared for them a city." Hebrews 11:15-16

The Bible says that if they put their minds where they had left, they would have had cause to go back. That is, the people who are heaven-bound will not be remembering and be boasting about their lives as unbelievers. They would not be saying for instance; "You are very lucky that I am now born again." If you had done this to me when I was not born again, you would have been dead by now. You just praise God that I am born again". They boast about their old lives. Any small thing you do, they would say: "Is this what you are going to do to me in this place? I am not coming here again. People don't even greet me. I am not coming again." To candidates who are heaven-bound, the will of God is natural. They do not have to be pressurized. at all. It becomes just a natural thing for them to do. Once God says something, that settles it. No matter their own opinion, they drop it.

2. **There is no way that earthly powers can harm them:**

"He that cometh from above is above all: he that is of the earth is earthly, and speaketh of the earth: he that cometh from heaven is above all." John 3:31

Those who are born again, have come from heaven, and there is no way the earthly can harm them. They are masters over witches, wizards, juju (charm), and all the powers of the herbalists. If you are afraid of juju, and of witches and wizards, I am unhappy to tell you that you are on your way to hell, because candidates for heaven don't suffer from such things. The Bible says that a sinner is running while no one is chasing him. Such is the lot of people who are candidates for hell.

3. **They are fools for Christ:**

"And an highway shall be there, and a way, and it shall be called the way of holiness; the unclean shall not pass over it; but it shall be for those: the way fairing men, though fools, shall not err therein." Isaiah 35: 8

They are fools for Christ. They are not wise in their own eyes, they are not wise in the deceit and the counsel of the world. That is why Peter in his first message, when he was preaching on the day of Pentecost, told the Jews that God came in the image of His Son, and that they killed Him by their wicked hands.

The Bible says that when they heard this, they were pricked to their heart, and they cried out: "Brethren, what shall we do?" Peter said, "Repent and be ye baptised, everyone of you, in the name of Jesus, and you shall receive the baptism of the Holy Ghost." The Bible says that with more words he exhorted them to save themselves from that crooked generation. If one is not careful about this generation, he will find himself where he does not want to go. By the way candidates for heaven dress, other people will call them foolish people. By the way they walk,
they would be called foolish people.

By the way they pray, they would be called foolish people. By the way they refuse to react when people want to make them angry they would be called foolish people. Many people abuse them but when they refuse to be angry, they call them fools. The Bible says, "Though they are fools, they will not miss it."

4. **They do not steal God's money:**

"Lay not up for yourselves treasures upon earth, where moth and rust doth corrupt, and where thieves break through and steal: But lay up for yourselves treasures in heaven, where neither moth nor rust doth corrupt, and where thieves

do not break through nor steal: For where your treasure is, there will your heart be also."
Matthew 6:19-21

So, the candidates for heaven will not steal God's money. They will give more than is required of them. Most believers today are not even giving enough. They are crying that they want financial breakthrough, can they get it when they are not giving? For the fact that you are hoarding money, the LORD allows devourers to take it away from you. You may spend 250 naira on one drug. Candidates for hell will always steal God's money for carnal purposes. Their hearts are where their money is. But those who are banking with God in heaven will go to heaven. So, think about this.

5. **They live holy lives, not dirty lives:**

"Follow peace with all men, and holiness, without which no man shall see the LORD." Hebrews 12:14

It does not say, "No man shall see miracles, but that no man shall see the LORD." It does not say that no man can see vision, or can prophesy, or can even see the supernatural power of God working, but that no man shall see the LORD without holiness. Think about this.

6. **They are already living in heaven now:** Some of the worldly songs that are in our hymn books should be deleted from there. A popular one says: "When I get home my sorrow will be over."

If it is not over here, it is not likely to be over when you get there. Believers are not supposed to be living carnally, but experiencing the life in heaven. If you are one to reign with

Jesus for 1000 years but you have never seen His pictures, you have never seen His angels, you are always seeing masquerades and you want to reign with Him, how will you do it? You ought to start living in that heaven now. 2 Corinthians 12:2-5 says,

"I knew a man in Christ above fourteen years ago, (whether in the body, I cannot tell; or whether out of the body, I cannot tell: God knoweth;) such an one caught up to the third heaven. And I knew such a man (whether in the body, or out of the body, I cannot tell: God knoweth;) How that he was caught up into paradise and heard unspeakable words, which it is not lawful for a man to utter. Of such one will I glory; yet of myself I will not glory but in mine infirmities."

Paul said, if you want to boast, that should be your boasting. Somebody who was alive was caught up to paradise to see what was happening there. Many believers are afraid of dying. It is necessary to find out from them where they want to go.

Apostle Paul says in Philippians 1:23, "For I am in a strait betwixt two, having a desire to depart, and to be with Christ, which is far better." Verse 24 says, "Nevertheless to abide in the flesh is more needful for you." So, the reason Paul was still alive was because he wanted to continue to minister to the people, not because he did not want to go to heaven. He was in a position to go or to stay. That was the life of somebody already living in the spirit.

Peter also knew when he was going to die. 2 Peter 1:14: "Knowing that shortly I must put to this my tabernacle, even as our Lord Jesus Christ hath showed me." He knew where he was going. There was a man of God in America called Godwin Peterson. As he was preaching one day he said: "Ladies and gentlemen, I am going home." They did not understand what he was saying. He went back to his seat, sat down and was gone. He knew when he was going to die. That was somebody living in the spirit.

Beloved, I want you to take a decision within you. Where are you heading for? Is it hell or heaven? If it is heaven, you have heard. The Bible says that precious is the death of the righteous. This means that some deaths are useless to God. You have to check up where you belong. If your mind is too much in the world, the world will hold you down here. But if your mind is in heaven, then that is where you are going. Have you been saying no to the voice of the Holy Spirit on the faults He has been pointing out in your life?

Where are you going? Religion cannot save you. You say you are confirmed in a church. Is there confirmation in the Bible? Can confirmation save you? If you have not repented and they baptised you, what happened was that you went into the pool as a dry sinner and came out as a wet sinner. There is therefore no difference between you and somebody who went to the swimming pool to have a bath. Church membership cannot save anybody.

Many people will discover that too late. "I belong to this, I belong to that," is not relevant to God at all. What is relevant to God is whether your name is in the Book of life. So, if now you have a feeling of secret, selfish pride, or pride about your position in life, you are not on your way to heaven. If you feel that an important and independent spirit is within you, or you are bitter over something that has passed which you cannot forgive, or you have no hunger for God at all or that anger is still stirring up inside your spirit, that your spirit is so sensitive and touchy, that people try to avoid you because they know you may spark off at any moment, or you have an unteachable spirit and you refuse to be taught, then you are not on your way to heaven. If you are always complaining or you like being noticed, you are not on your way to heaven. Or are you compromising your faith because of money? Are you so unstable in the faith and you are afraid of God, of Christ and of the Bible? Do you love human praise and find fault with every other person? Or do you criticise things that you cannot do well? Think about all these.

The rich man prayed too late. He prayed to father Abraham: "Let someone go unto them from the dead and they will repent." Abraham refused to ask God to send back people from the dead. We are very fortunate in this country. God has been generous to us. He has been sending back people from the dead to talk to people here. It is not even enough to say, "I believe God," or "My heart is clean." The Bible says, "Thou believest that there is one God, thou doest well, for the devil also believeth and he trembles." Evil spirits have a strong malice against the children of men. They know that they are going to hell fire, and they don't like the idea that sons of men are going to heaven. They don't like the fact that hell fire was not created for man, but for the devil and his angels. I remember the story of that man who wanted to steal a goat. He took his four children and said to them: "You hide there, you hide by my left, you hide at my back, you hide by my right. If you see anybody coming, give me a sign that I will quickly stop whatever I 'm doing. "But as he moved to catch the goat, one of the children exclaimed, "Papa, wait, wait." The man said, "What is the matter? Is somebody coming?" The child said, "No, who is watching this way?" He pointed to the sky. In other words the father had taken care of the north, east, south and west but the small child pointed to and asked about heaven? How about God? Does He not see you? The man left the goat. Those of us who think we can hide anything from God deceive ourselves.

It is not a sign of spiritual maturity when you are living above your experience, and you refuse to call the LORD to deliver you when you need deliverance. Do you say no to Jesus? It is time for you to repent. The invisible hand of death can come at any time. That somebody is healthy at night does not mean that he will wake up the next morning. The thought that there is no visible danger does not mean there is security.

The arrows of death are flying morning, noon and night. The sharpest eyes cannot see them. Unbelievers and sinners are walking over the pit of hell fire. The pit may collapse at any time. The Bible says we brought nothing to this world, and it is certain that nobody will go with anything.

One woman died in America at a time she had 10, 000 dresses in her wardrobe. When her relatives auctioned the dresses, they made 40, 000 dollars. But do you know how many of the dresses they used for her burial? Three! Out of the 10, 000 dresses. Think about this.

> *"Be not thou afraid when one is made rich, when the glory of his house is increased; for when he dieth, he shall carry nothing away: his glory shall not descend after him."* Psalm 49:16

PRAYER POINTS

1. Father Lord, deliver me from carnality so that the flesh will not destroy me, in Jesus' name.

2. Father Lord, cut away from me all the chains and stings of iniquity, in Jesus' name.

3. Spirit of the living God, fall afresh upon me, in the name of Jesus. Father Lord, restore to me all my blessings that I have lost through sin, in the name of Jesus.

OTHER BOOKS BY DR. D. K. OLUKOYA

1. 20 Marching Orders To Fulfill Your Destiny
2. A-Z of Complete Deliverance
3. Abraham's Children in Bondage
4. Be Prepared
5. Bewitchment must die
6. Biblical Principles of Dream Interpretation
7. Born Great, But Tied Down
8. Breaking Bad Habits
9. Breakthrough Prayers For Business Professionals
10. Brokenness
11. Bringing Down The Power of God
12. Can God?
13. Can God Trust You?
14. Command The Morning
15. Consecration Commitment & Loyalty
16. Contending For The Kingdom
17. Connecting to The God of Breakthroughs
18. Criminals In The House Of God
19. Dancers At The Gate of Death
20. Dealing With Hidden Curses
21. Dealing With Local Satanic Technology
22. Dealing With Satanic Exchange
23. Dealing With The Evil Powers Of Your Father's House
24. Dealing With Tropical Demons
25. Dealing With Unprofitable Roots
26. Dealing With Witchcraft Barbers
27. Deliverance By Fire
28. Deliverance From Spirit Husband And Spirit Wife
29. Deliverance From The Limiting Powers
30. Deliverance of The Brain
31. Deliverance Of The Conscience

32. Deliverance Of The Head
33. Deliverance: God's Medicine Bottle
34. Destiny Clinic
35. Destroying Satanic Masks
36. Disgracing Soul Hunters
37. Divine Military Training
38. Divine Yellow Card
39. Dominion Prosperity
40. Drawers Of Power From The Heavenlies
41. Evil Appetite
42. Evil Umbrella
43. Facing Both Ways
44. Failure In The School Of Prayer
45. Fire For Life's Journey
46. For We Wrestle ...
47. Freedom Indeed
48. Holiness Unto The Lord
49. Holy Cry
50. Holy Fever
51. Hour Of Decision
52. How To Obtain Personal Deliverance
53. How To Pray When Surrounded By The Enemies
54. Idols Of The Heart
55. Is This What They Died For?
56. Let God Answer By Fire
57. Lord, Behold Their Threatening
58. Limiting God
59. Madness Of The Heart
60. Making Your Way Through The Traffic Jam of Life
61. Meat For Champions
62. Medicine For Winners
63. My Burden For The Church
64. Open Heavens Through Holy Disturbance

65. Overpowering Witchcraft
66. Paralysing The Riders And The Horse
67. Personal Spiritual Check-Up
68. Possessing The Tongue of Fire
69. Power Against Coffin Spirits
70. Power Against Destiny Quenchers
71. Power Against Dream Criminals
72. Power Against Local Wickedness
73. Power Against Marine Spirits
74. Power Against Spiritual Terrorists
75. Power To Recover Your Lost Glory
76. Power Must Change Hands
77. Pray Your Way To Breakthroughs
78. Prayer Is The Battle
79. Prayer Rain
80. Prayer Strategies For Spinsters And Bachelors
81. Prayer To Kill Enchantment
82. Prayer To Make You Fulfill Your Divine Destiny
83. Prayer Warfare Against 70 Mad Spirits
84. Prayers For Open Heavens
85. Prayers To Destroy Diseases And Infirmities
86. Prayers To Move From Minimum To Maximum
87. Praying Against The Spirit Of The Valley
88. Praying To Destroy Satanic Roadblocks
89. Praying To Dismantle Witchcraft
90. Principles Of Prayer
91. Release From Destructive Covenants
92. Revoking Evil Decrees
93. Safeguarding Your Home
94. Satanic Diversion Of The Black Race
95. Seventy Sermons To Preach To Your Destiny
96. Silencing The Birds Of Darkness
97. Slaves Who Love Their Chains

98. Smite The Enemy And He Will Flee
99. Speaking Destruction Unto The Dark Rivers
100. Spiritual Education
101. Spiritual Growth And Maturity
102. Spiritual Warfare And The Home
103. Strategic Praying
104. Strategy Of Warfare Praying
105. Stop Them Before They Stop You
106. Students In The School Of Fear
107. Symptoms Of Witchcraft Attack
108. The Baptism of Fire
109. The Battle Against The Spirit Of Impossibility
110. The Dinning Table Of Darkness
111. The Enemy Has Done This
112. The Evil Cry Of Your Family Idol
113. The Fire Of Revival
114. The Great Deliverance
115. The Internal Stumbling Block
116. The Lord Is A Man Of War
117. The Mystery Of Mobile Curses
118. The Mystery Of The Mobile Temple
119. The Prayer Eagle
120. The Power of Aggressive Prayer Warriors
121. The Pursuit Of Success
122. The Seasons Of Life
123. The Secrets Of Greatness
124. The Serpentine Enemies
125. The Skeleton In Your Grandfather's Cupboard
126. The Slow Learners
127. The Snake In The Power House
128. The Spirit Of The Crab
129. The star hunters
130. The Star In Your Sky

131. The Terrible Agenda
132. The Tongue Trap
133. The Unconquerable Power
134. The Unlimited God
135. The Vagabond Spirit
136. The Way Of Divine Encounter
137. The Wealth Transfer Agenda
138. Tied Down In The Spirits
139. Too Hot To Handle
140. Turnaround Breakthrough
141. Unprofitable Foundations
142. Vacancy For Mad Prophets
143. Victory Over Satanic Dreams
144. Victory Over Your Greatest Enemies
145. Violent Prayers Against Stubborn Situations
146. War At The Edge Of Breakthroughs
147. Wasting The Wasters
148. Wealth Must Change Hands
149. What You Must Know About The House Fellowship
150. When God Is Silent
151. When the Battle is from Home
152. When The Deliverer Need Deliverance
153. When Things Get Hard
154. When You Are Knocked Down
155. Where Is Your Faith
156. While Men Slept
157. Woman! Thou Art Loosed.
158. Your Battle And Your Strategy
159. Your Foundation And Destiny
160. Your Mouth And Your Deliverance

YORUBA PUBLICATIONS

1. ADURA AGBAYORI

2. ADURA TI NSI OKE NIDI

3. OJO ADURA

FRENCH PUBLICATIONS

1. PLUIE DE PRIERE
2. ESPIRIT DE VAGABONDAGE
3. EN FINIR AVEC LES FORCES MALEFIQUES DE LA MAISON DE TON PERE
4. QUE l'ENVOUTEMENT PERISSE
5. FRAPPEZ l'ADVERSAIRE ET IL FUIRA
6. COMMENT RECEVIR LA DELIVRANCE DU MARI ET FEMME DE NUIT
7. CPMMENT SE DELIVRER SOI-MEME
8. POVOIR CONTRE LES TERRORITES SPIRITUEL
9. PRIERE DE PERCEES POUR LES HOMMES D'AFFAIRES
10. PRIER JUSQU'A REMPORTER LA VICTOIRE
11. PRIERES VIOLENTES POUR HUMILIER LES PROBLEMES OPINIATRES
12. PRIERE POUR DETRUIRE LES MALADIES ET INFIRMITES
13. LE COMBAT SPIRITUEL ET LE FOYER
14. BILAN SPIRITUEL PERSONNEL
15. VICTOIRES SUR LES REVES SATANIQUES
16. PRIERES DE COMAT CONTRE 70 ESPIRITS DECHANINES
17. LA DEVIATION SATANIQUE DE LA RACE NOIRE
18. TON COMBAT ET TA STRATEGIE
19. VOTRE FONDEMENT ET VOTRE DESTIN
20. REVOQUER LES DECRETS MALEFIQUES
21. CANTIQUE DES CONTIQUES
22. LE MAUVAIS CRI DES IDOLES
23. QUAND LES CHOSES DEVIENNENT DIFFICILES
24. LES STRATEGIES DE PRIERES POUR LES CELIBATAIRES
25. SE LIBERER DES ALLIANCES MALEFIQUES
26. DEMANTELER LA SORCELLERIE
27. LA DELIVERANCE: LE FLACON DE MEDICAMENT DIEU
28. LA DELIVERANCE DE LA TETE
29. COMMANDER LE MATIN
30. NE GRAND MAIS LIE
31. POUVOIR CONTRE LESDEMOND TROPICAUX
32. LE PROGRAMME DE TRANFERT DE RICHESSE
33. LES ETUDIANTS A l'ECOLE DE LA PEUR
34. L'ETOILE DANS VOTRE CIEL
35. LES SAISONS DE LA VIE
36. FEMME TU ES LIBEREE

ANNUAL 70 DAYS PRAYER AND FASTING PUBLICATIONS

1. Prayers That Bring Miracles
2. Let God Answer By Fire
3. Prayers To Mount With Wings As Eagles
4. Prayers That Bring Explosive Increase
5. Prayers For Open Heavens
6. Prayers To Make You Fulfil Your Divine Destiny
7. Prayers That Make God To Answer And Fight By Fire
8. Prayers That Bring Unchallengeable Victory And Breakthrough Rainfall Bombardments
9. Prayers That Bring Dominion Prosperity And Uncommon Success
10. Prayers That Bring Power And Overflowing Progress
11. Prayers That Bring Laughter And Enlargement Breakthroughs
12. Prayers That Bring Uncommon Favour And Breakthroughs
13. Prayers That Bring Unprecedented Greatness & Unmatchable Increase
14. Prayers That Bring Awesome Testimonies And Turn Around Breakthroughs

www.ingramcontent.com/pod-product-compliance
Lightning Source LLC
Chambersburg PA
CBHW071957070426
42453CB00008BA/988